The Most Difficult Decisions You'll Never Have to Make

Would you rather...
never be able to experience orgasm
OR
perpetually experience orgasm?

Would you rather...
have mayonnaise tears
OR
Koolaid sweat?

Would you rather...
sleep a night on a bed of peanut butter
OR
next to a humidifier full of urine?

Would you rather...
worms for eyelashes
OR
corduroy skin?

Would you rather...
have a tape-dispensing mouth
OR
bottle opening nostrils?

Would you rather...
have your Lamaze coach be Marv Albert
OR
the guy from Police Academy who made all those crazy sound effects?

Would you rather...?®
THE ULTIMATE CHALLENGE

YOU MUST CHOOSE
**Over 700 Absolutely
Absurd Dilemmas To Ponder**

Justin Heimberg • David Gomberg

METRO BOOKS
NEW YORK

Acknowledgments

We'd like to recognize the contributions and help of Steve Harwood, Jonah Van Zandt, Chris Schultz, Todd DeHart, Steve A, Paul Katz, Jeff Sank, Jason Heimberg, Matt Scharf, Chris DeSena, Dave Miller, Dan Binstock, Bob Bernstein, Kert "Coach" Mease, Todd Wagnon, Darren A. LaVarne, Grimaldi, Boesch, Eric Gomberg, Nicky Siegel, Brian "Sugar Daddy" Sugar, Dan "The Man" Levitan, Jon Mirsky, Aaron Hilliard, Kit Pongetti, Charlie Kranz, Joliene Hamodot, Lizbet Traks, Megan Incorvaia, Rick Foss, Steve Wallace and anyone else who sent us questions that we unconsciously stole. Thanks to all the *WYR* fans for your support.

Thank you to Davey-Boy Smith for your business casual acumen. Thanks to Jay Mandel for believing in all of our delusions. Thanks to Tom Schirtz—we are all mere pawns of your Design.

Gomberg: While I'll never be able to compete with the Great Kabuki's in-the-ring prowess, you still found a way to fall in love with me. Sophia, you are my wife and my life.

Heimberg: Thank you, Marisa, for giving me a reason to retire that ten year old forlorn author photo. I promise some day I'll have a real book to dedicate to you. I love you.

"This is a book I do not show my rabbi." —David Gomberg

A Note from the Authors

As the ten year anniversary of the original *Would You Rather...?* nears, we are reminded of the great Leonard Nimoy whose book *I Am Not Spock*, written to separate the author's identity from the eponymous character, was followed by a sequel *I Am Spock*, in which Nimoy essentially conceded he was Spock after all. So we feel is the case with us and *Would You Rather...?* Despite Heimberg's tenure rehabilitating at-risk youth through poetry and Gomberg's venture into competitive origami—we are still labeled "the Would You Rather guys" a title which neither makes for a good wrestling tag-team nor gets you laid.

After several more futile attempts to redefine ourselves, including a stint as a White Lion cover band, we finally concluded, "Why fight it, anymore?" Why not instead embrace the power of recycled content? Why not assemble the infantile, puerile, juvenile questions into one superlative tome of time-wasting absurdity?

So then, please enjoy this collection of the best *Would You Rather...?*® questions culled from our various works, supplemented with all new, never-seen-before questions.

We are Spock.

Table of Contents

How to use this book

Sit around with a bunch of friends and read a question to each other, discussing it until the momentum of the conversation fades into awkward stares and glances. Everybody must choose. As the deity proclaims, **YOU MUST CHOOSE!** That's the whole premise of this thing. It forces you to really think about the options. Once everyone has chosen, move on to the next question. It's that simple. We have provided a few things to consider when deliberating each question, but don't restrict yourself to these, as much of the fun comes from imagining the different ways your choice will affect your life.

Whether played with friends or used as bathroom literary fodder, (or both if you have an extremely open and intimate circle of friends) *Would Your Rather...?* will make you laugh, make you think, and make you very confused. So turn the page, read on, and embarrass yourself by mumbling in public "I could have done this. Damn it, why didn't I think of this? I could have made so much money. Damn it!"

CHAPTER 1
CURSED AGAIN

These are the circumstances. A deity descends from on high and informs you that, for reasons beyond your understanding, your life is about to change. You are to be stricken with a terrible curse—a bizarre behavioral disorder, a peculiar physical deformity, an infuriating inconvenience, etc.—the details of which are limited only by this sick-minded god-thing's imagination. You need not feel entirely powerless, however. The Deity allows you to choose between two possible fates.

YOU MUST CHOOSE!

Would you rather...

have an 8 inch wide innie belly-button

OR

have a 10 inch long outie belly button?

Would you rather...

make the sounds of the Bionic Man when straining physically

OR

make the sound of the *Jeopardy* theme when straining mentally?

Things to consider: test-taking, gym class

Would you rather...

be compelled to enter every room by jumping into the doorway with an imaginary pistol drawn like the star of a 70's cop show

OR

invariably make your orgasm face instead of smiling when being photographed?

Would you rather...

cough the sound of bagpipes

OR

fart the sound of a rapid-fire machine gun?

CURSED AGAIN

YOU MUST CHOOSE!

Would you rather be a Siamese twin...

connected at the soles of your feet *OR* at the lips?

by the finger tips *OR* by the hair?

at the buttocks *OR* at the elbows/knees?

your feet on your twin's shoulders *OR* his/her feet on yours?

with Joey Lawrence *OR* Kareem Abdul-Jabbar?

Would you rather...

have bacon bit dandruff

OR

have the voice in your head sound like Jimmy Stewart?

Would you rather...

have fingernails that grow at a rate of one inch per minute

OR

have pubic hair that grows at the same rate?

Things to consider: putting in contact lenses, sex life, tanning at the beach

Would you rather...

be 50 pounds heavier and look it

OR

300 pounds heavier but look the same as you do now?

CURSED AGAIN

YOU MUST CHOOSE!

Would you rather...

have lit candle wicks for hair *OR* asparagus for fingers?

worms for eyelashes *OR* corduroy skin?

a pair of oversized dice for an Adam's apple *OR* Ralph Lauren Polo logos for nipples?

Would you rather...

have glow-in-the-dark veins

OR

have red smoke perpetually leaking from your nostrils?

Would you rather have a tattoo of...

various geometric formulas *OR* all the vice presidents' heads?

the faces of Bartles and Jaymes on each kneecap *OR* an extension of your ass crack on your lower back?

a scratch-and-sniff tattoo of a pickle *OR* a tattoo consisting of the Chinese character for "trite?"

Would you rather...

have mood lips (change color according to your mood)

OR

make the sound of the shaking of Boggle letter cubes when laughing?

CURSED AGAIN

YOU MUST CHOOSE!

Would you rather...
have a horizontal buttcrack

OR

vertically aligned breasts?

Would you rather...
have your eyes always moving as if watching a ping-pong match

OR

speak in the voice, volume, and intensity of a screaming Janis Joplin when speaking to anyone under 7 years old?

Would you rather...

have a written lisp

OR

fizz up like Alka-Seltzer when in the water?

Things to consider: thwimming

Would you rather...

have to have sex in the same position every night

OR

have to have sex in a different position every night (you can never repeat)?

Things to consider: cowgirl, reverse cowgirl, pile driver, reverse pile driver, doggie-style, penguin-style, missionary, rabbinical missionary, the startled spelunker, the Van Zandt spin, 69, 96, 55, 127, 00 (aka the Robert Parish)?

YOU MUST CHOOSE!

Would you rather...

have 14 navels *OR* 24 toes?

6 lips *OR* 34 fingers?

1 nostril *OR* 8 nostrils?

15 fingers *OR* 3 tongues?

no nipples *OR* 11 nipples?

17 testicles *OR* one extremely restless one?

Things to consider: Reread now as "Would you rather date someone who had..."

Would you rather...

everything you say be considered an insult

OR

a come-on?

Would you rather...

speak to the tune of Village People songs

OR

have your sole means of locomotion be breakdancing?
Things to consider: What's the past tense of breakdance? Brokedance?
Breakdanced?

Would you rather...

have a comic book-style thought bubble

OR

a comic book-style dialogue bubble?
Things to consider: loss of privacy, hiding your thoughts with a big hat, ability
to converse with the deaf, inability to converse with the blind

---

YOU MUST CHOOSE!

Would you rather...

have invisible skin

OR

see in strobe light?

Things to consider: evening commute, modeling for biology text books

Would you rather...

have an intense urge to whisper sweet nothings into the ears of bus drivers as you pay your fare

OR

have parents who affectionately refer to you as "anal cakes"?

Things to consider: teacher-parent conferences, wedding toasts

Would you rather always have to wear...

pants four sizes too small *OR* ten-inch high heels?

a tight tube top that says "bad girl" *OR* used tea bag earrings?

acid wash jeans *OR* the male perm?

hot pants *OR* a parrot?

NFL referee garb *OR* a wizard's robe and hat?

Miller's outfits from ninth grade *OR* DeSena's outfits now?

YOU MUST CHOOSE!

Would you rather...

have permanent Cheetoh residue on your fingertips

OR

appear as Shemp of The Three Stooges in all photographs?

Things to consider: wedding pictures, typing

Would you rather...

have anti-gravity hair

OR

have all your dreams written and directed by the guys who made those blacksploitation films of the 70's?

YOU MUST CHOOSE!

Would you rather...

speak in the voice of a possessed Linda Blair in *The Exorcist* whenever talking to cashiers and retail workers

OR

have "Starbucks Tourettes" where you randomly exclaim Starbucks orders? (for example... "Hi, How are --- Double Decaf Iced Mocha Frap!")

Would you rather...

have a nose that pulsates like a human heart

OR

be allowed to use only toothpaste for all hygiene purposes/processes?

CURSED AGAIN

YOU MUST CHOOSE!

Would you rather...

snore the sound of a dial up modem

OR

be allergic to smooth jazz?

Would you rather...

have a rare disorder that allows you to dispose of bodily waste only in pool table pockets

OR

ever so slowly morph into Bob Barker as you age?

Hostage Crisis

These are the circumstances: You have been taken hostage by a group of militant terrorists (They work for the deity). The terrorists' leader says he will allow the US government to send one person in to negotiate your fate.

Would you rather your hostage negotiator be...

Dick Vitale *OR* Ike Turner?

Ozzy Osbourne *OR* Jessica Simpson?

Jimmy Carter *OR* Pamela Anderson?

the host of "Mad Money" *OR* Marcel Marceau?

Phil Bautista *OR* "The American Dream" Dusty Rhodes?

CURSED AGAIN

YOU MUST CHOOSE!

Interior Motives

The Deity is into Anti-Feng-Shui, the ancient Japanese art of the disharmonious placement and arrangement of objects in a given space. With this in mind, he decides your home needs some shaping up.

Would you rather...

have American cheese linens

OR

wall to wall ground beef carpet?

Would you rather...

have *Prince Valiant* comic strip wallpaper

OR

Willis Reed permanently residing on your loveseat?

CHAPTER 2
SEX

Like the deities and demi-gods of the Greeks, this is a god concerned with the earthly delights of hedonism. Perhaps "concerned" is not a strong enough word. Obsessed. Morbidly. Particularly in the comings and goings of his pet mortals. And so, for these reasons, and others beyond your understanding, he feels that your sex life could be so much more interesting.

YOU MUST CHOOSE!

Would you rather...

have your genitalia located on the top of your head

OR

the bottom of your left foot?

Things to consider: jogging, hats, the sexual act, masturbation

Would you rather...

have a permanent smile

OR

a permanent erection?

Things to consider: church, visiting grandma, funerals

Would you rather...

have commercial interruptions during masturbation fantasies

OR

have to masturbate with the mandatory use of a Sesame Street's Elmo hand puppet?

Would you rather...

see in ColecoVision graphics quality when having sex

OR

have to use clinical terms during dirty talk? (for example, "Penetrate that vagina!" ; "Lick that mons pubis!"; "Ram that glans against the epidermis of the uvula!")

SEX

YOU MUST CHOOSE!

Would you rather...

always orgasm thirty seconds into sex

OR

only be able to orgasm after three hours of continuous sex?

Would you rather...

have your range of sexual body movement equal to that of a He-Man doll

OR

speak like Yoda when attracted to someone?

Would you rather...

have genitalia that reduces in size two percent each time it is used

OR

genitalia that increases in size twenty-five percent each time it is used?

Would you rather...

have orgasms that feel like a brain-freeze

OR

be able to maintain an erection (men)/reach orgasm (women) only by accurately reciting the digits of Pi (you have to start over if you mess up)?

Things to consider:

3.14159265358979323846264338327950288419716939937510582097494459230781
6406286208998628034825342117067982148086513282306647093844609550582
2317253594081284811174502841027019385211055596446229489549303819 6442...

SEX

YOU MUST CHOOSE!

Would you rather have sex with...

Hillary Clinton *OR* Natalie from *Facts of Life*?

Oprah *OR* Rosie?

Jessica Rabbit *OR* Daphne from *Scooby Doo*?

Connie Chung *OR* a 200% enlarged Halle Berry?

Venus Williams *OR* Sheryl Crow if she spoke in the voice of an old Jewish man?

A "10" *OR* five "2's"? (At the same time)?

Would you rather have sex with...

Bryant Gumble *OR* "Weird" Al Yankovic?

Alex Trebec *OR* Larry David?

Yao Ming *OR* Mini-me from *Austin Powers*?

Johnny Depp without a leg *OR* Tom Selleck without a moustache?

Matt Damon *OR* Ben Affleck?

Matt Damon *OR* Ben Affleck if they exchanged heights?

S E X

YOU MUST CHOOSE!

During sex, would you rather...

utter all exclamations in the computerized voice of Stephen Hawking

OR

compulsively compliment yourself?

Would you rather...

be able to have sex exclusively with palindromes

OR

only be able to masturbate to the two wise-ass critics in the *Muppet Show*?

Things to consider: Lil, Anna, Otto, race car

Would you rather...

orgasm once every ten years

OR

once every ten seconds?

Things to consider: business meetings, funerals, public speaking

During sex, would you rather hear...

"Uh-oh" *OR* "What is that?!"?

"Oops" *OR* "That's where that is"?

a yawn *OR* "Oy Vey"?

nervous laughter *OR* maniacal laughter?

"Must kill president" *OR* "Circuit malfunction"?

S E X

YOU MUST CHOOSE!

Would you rather have sex with...

Meg Ryan and lose your sense of smell

OR

Janet Reno and earn the official title of "Commandant"?

Would you rather have sex with...

Matthew McConnohangy and lose a finger

OR

Burt Reynolds and learn how to properly spell "McConaughey"?

Would you rather have phone sex with...

the narrator of all those movie trailers *OR* Alf?

Hardball's Chris Matthews *OR* Donald Trump?

Ernest Hemmingway *OR* Dr. Seuss?

Yoda *OR* Bob Ross (the calm "Happy Trees" painter from PBS)?

a severe stutterer *OR* someone who has a sexy voice but uses fifth grade terms like "boobie," "tushy," "pee-pee," and "bagina" for sex words?

Elrond *OR* the character from the old Snausages commercials?

S E X

YOU MUST CHOOSE!

Would you rather have sex with...

Russell Crowe *OR* Pierce Brosnan?

Johnny Depp *OR* George Clooney?

Clay Aiken *OR* Ruben Studdard?

C3PO *OR* R2D2?

Would you rather have sex with...

Gwen Stefani *OR* Jennifer Aniston?

Cameron Diaz *OR* Jennifer Love Hewitt?

the new Daisy Duke (Jessica Simpson) *OR* classic Daisy Duke (Catherine Bach)?

Rebecca Romijn *OR* Rebecca Romijn-Stamos?

Would you rather have...

(women, read the following questions as "have a partner with")

a two-pronged penis OR a penis that bends at a right angle in the middle?

a penis that turns green and tears out of your clothing like the Incredible Hulk every time you get aroused OR an invisible penis?

a Rubik's Snake penis OR a penis that can act as a light saber upon your command?

Would you...

dry hump Leonard Nimoy to gain complete knowledge of the "V" encyclopedia?

Things to consider: Vermont, Vatican City, Vulcans

S E X

YOU MUST CHOOSE!

Would you rather your only porn be...

6 second clips of hot people *OR* 2 minute clips of moderately attractive people?

verbose, subtle erotic fiction *OR* pornographic Magic Eye 3D pictures (the ones where you have to stare just right until the image comes into focus)?

Spanish channel variety shows *OR* vague, slightly inaccurate recollections of a 1980's Markie Post?

animal nature documentaries *OR* suggestive cloud formations?

geometric shapes *OR* family reunion pictures?
Things to consider: the arousing rhombus

Would you rather...

your penis (men)/breasts (women) increase in size by ten percent each year

OR

decrease in size by two percent each year?

Would you rather...

vicariously experience all orgasms that occur in your zip code

OR

during sex, have the Microsoft paper clip help icon appear with sex tips?

S E X

YOU MUST CHOOSE!

The Deity has always been one to fuel sibling rivalry.

Would you rather have sex with...

Alec *OR* Billy Baldwin?

Fred *OR* Ben Savage?

Orville *OR* Wilbur Wright?

Things to consider: Wilbur was hung like a Shetland pony.

Would you rather...

have to call your parents and ask for permission every time you have sex

OR

be mandated to perform all sexual activity to Denise Williams' "Let's Hear it for the Boy"?

WOULD YOU RATHER...?

Would you rather...

have a lover who is 6' tall with a 2 inch penis

OR

4' tall with a 12 inch penis?

3' tall with a 16 inch penis?

2' tall with a 26 inch penis?

Would you rather...

ejaculate guacamole *OR* Tabasco sauce?

Scope *OR* crazy string?

air-rifle bb's *OR* high voltage electric shocks?

Bee Gee's music *OR* baseball umpire strike and ball calls?

through your nostrils *OR* through your eyes?

SEX

YOU MUST CHOOSE!

Would you rather have a lover with measurements...

36-26-36 *OR* 33-23-34?

44-28-40 *OR* 34-18-30?

100-100-100 *OR* 36-24-36-26-58?

5-286-3 *OR* 38-26-44

(not necessarily in that order; measurements constantly shift)

Would you rather...

have Angelina Jolie as your personal sex slave *OR* an unlimited supply of pork? Jolie as your sex slave *OR* unlimited pork and season tickets to all sporting events? Jolie as your sex slave *OR* the pork, season tickets, and a personal minstrel who records your deeds in song?

Would you rather...

have joy buzzers built into your breasts

OR

have your g-spot located under your right armpit?
In your left nostril?
In the lunch box of a fifth grader in Milwaukee, Wisconsin?

Would you rather...

have an intense spotlight perpetually shining from your crotch

OR

have your partner appear as Mao Tse-tung during sex?
Things to consider: receiving oral sex

S E X

YOU MUST CHOOSE!

Would you rather have sex with...

A 60% scale Jennifer Aniston *OR* a winged Kate Hudson?

Meryl Streep *OR* a severely jaundiced Britney Spears?

A profusely sweating Deborah Norville *OR* a butter-soaked Margot Kidder?

A three way with Cameron Diaz and Tim Russert *OR* Lucy Liu and Gandalf?

Would you rather have sex with...

Randy Quaid *OR* an Indian version of Viggo Mortensen?

A soft and gentle Ted Koppel *OR* a fast and furious Pillsbury Dough Boy?

A three way with J-Lo and Alan Greenspan *OR* Shakira and the Hamburglar?
Things to consider: Robble, Robble

Would you rather...

have a retractable penis

OR

a detachable scrotum (patent pending)?

Would you rather...

have your sexual partner suddenly transported to New Orleans upon your achieving climax

OR

have your sexual exploits narrated and commented upon by the bodyless voices of Al Michaels and John Madden?

Things to consider: one night stands, spite sex, Michaels and Madden's charming rapport

SEX

YOU MUST CHOOSE!

Would you rather...

attract swarms of fireflies when aroused

OR

have the sound of microphone feedback intermittently emanating from your crotch?

Would you rather...

have gratuitous Ted Danson cameos during erotic dreams

OR

be able to only have sex on bumper pool tables?

Would you rather have...

(women, read the following questions as "have a partner with")

a 4 inch long penis with a 2 inch diameter OR an 8 inch penis with a half inch diameter?

a penis able to drink like an elephant uses his trunk OR a penis that glows in the dark when you twist the head?

Would you rather...

wear your pubic hair in a Fu-Manchu style OR ZZ Top beard style?

have pubic hair in the style of princess Leia's hair OR pubes comprised of Brillo?

have pubes that lit up like fiber optic wires OR pubes that grow "up" and around your body like ivy on a house?

S E X

YOU MUST CHOOSE!

Would you rather...

see an opera based on your love life

OR

a porno based on your sex life?

Would you rather...

utter all exclamations during sex in Shakespeare speak

OR

Haiku?

Things to Consider:

    oh yeah do me yeah

    like willow reed in cool pond

    pinch my nipple

When you sleep, would you rather...

instead of REM (rapid eye movement), experience WTL (wild tongue lapping) *OR* have your penis move like a windshield wiper?

be a sleepwalker *OR* a sleephumper?

experience nocturnal tumescence *OR* nocturnal luminescence?

Would you rather...

receive a Cleveland Steamer from Tom Snyder

OR

a Dirty Sanchez from former Postmaster General Marvin Runyon?

SEX

YOU MUST CHOOSE!

Would you rather...

receive oral sex from the subject in Edvard Munch's "The Scream"

OR

commit lewd acts on Teddy Ruxpin?

Would you rather...

have a website broadcast all your showers

OR

your bowel movements?

Would you rather have sex with...

Gwyneth Paltrow *OR* Carmen Electra with a unibrow?

a toothless Kelly Clarkson *OR* a hairless Thandie Newton?

Heidi Klum *OR* a threesome with Natalie Portman and her clone?

an albino Eva Longoria *OR* Katie Holmes slathered in mayo?

Lindsey Lohan 30 years from now *OR* Lindsey Lohan 6 years ago?

Elizabeth Hurley without the accent *OR* Beyoncé Knowles without the accent (i.e. Beyonce Knowles)?

S E X

YOU MUST CHOOSE!

This or That?

Challenge yourself or your friends with the following quiz.

Answers on page 239

1. Famous Children's Book *OR* Nazi Nickname?
   - a. The Desert Fox
   - b. The Velveteen Rabbit
   - c. The Angel of Death
   - d. Super Fudge

2. NHL team *OR* Historical Occurrence?
   - a. Colorado Avalanche
   - b. Missouri Compromise
   - c. Gadsden Purchase
   - d. St. Louis Blues

3a. Porn star *OR* meteorological term?

     a. Summer Cummings

     b. Winter Solstice

     c. Jet Stream

     d. Busty Dusty

3b. Meteorologist *OR* Porn Term?

     a. Flip Spiceland

     b. Pearl Necklace

     c. Al Roker

SEX

YOU MUST CHOOSE!

4. Jessica Tandy film *OR* euphemism for masturbation?
     a. Guarding Tess
     b. Choking The Chicken
     c. Driving Miss Daisy
     d. Polishing the Purple Army Helmet

5. Famous Indian Chieftain *OR* Euphemism for White Basketball Player?
     a. Sitting Bull
     b. Does-all-the-intangibles
     c. Shows-up-every-night
     d. Paula Poundstone

CHAPTER 3
NOT-QUITE-SUPER-POWERS

Lucky you. The Deity is in good spirits. Turns out, he was right all along. It is spelled "deity," not "diety." He's bubbling over with happiness, and wants to share it with you by bestowing upon you one of two peculiar, if not, super powers. Take your pick.

YOU MUST CHOOSE!

Would you rather...

have the ability to empty your bladder by "beaming" your urine to a toilet like in *Star Trek*

OR

be capable of shooting pubic "quills" in self-defense like a porcupine?

Would you rather...

be able to simulate the voice of anybody you meet

OR

simulate the hair?

Would you rather...

have Bettie Davis eyes

OR

Charles Manson eyes?

Would you rather...

be able to achieve orgasm at will

OR

be able to make anyone other than you achieve orgasm at your will?

Things to consider: public speakers, staff meetings, sporting events

NOT-QUITE-SUPER-POWERS

YOU MUST CHOOSE!

Would you rather...

have a tape-dispensing mouth

OR

bottle opening nostrils?

Would you rather...

have Spanish subtitles appear as you speak

OR

have a photographic memory where all the people involved are replaced with the cast of *Night Court*?

Things to Consider: Bull

Would you rather...

be able to consume fatty foods without gaining weight

OR

be able to have unprotected sex without getting sexual diseases?

Things to consider: Syphilis, Chlamydia, hot fudge, gravy fries, cheese balls

Would you rather...

be able to communicate with animals, but only the nerds

OR

be able to read people's minds but only when they are thinking about aluminum siding topics and issues?

NOT-QUITE-SUPER-POWERS

YOU MUST CHOOSE!

Would you rather...

have taste buds all over your body

OR

have a malleable stress-ball head?

Would you rather...

have an anus that can function as a DustBuster

or

nipples that can act as universal light dimmers?

Would you rather...

have a tongue that doubles as a retractable tape measure

OR

have a GPS built into your crotch?

Would you rather...

have an ever-changing tattoo that takes the form of whatever image you will it to be

OR

be able to psychically see anybody's internet browser history when looking at them?

NOT-QUITE-SUPER-POWERS

YOU MUST CHOOSE!

Would you rather...

have puma-like reactions with the remote control when watching something dirty, and someone walks into the room, and you need to change it

OR

have expert precision with the cheek-kiss greeting?

Would you rather...

have a stable of remarkably sympathetic woodland creatures to confide in about romantic desires and dreams

OR

be capable of ending any relationship tension-free with no ensuing debate or discussion by pulling out a red card like in soccer?

Things to consider: yellow card warnings

WOULD YOU RATHER...?

Would you rather...

have an ass-fax *OR* a Phillips head screwdriver outie belly button?

elastic lips *OR* reflective calves?

inflatable breasts *OR* adjustable palm lines?

Things to consider: messing with psychics

Would you rather...

be able to fast-forward life

OR

rewind it?

Things to consider: pelbin

YOU MUST CHOOSE!

Would you rather...

have the ability to talk clearly while dentists are working on your teeth

OR

permission to talk dirty?

Would you rather have your eulogy delivered by...

Jesse Jackson *OR* Bill O'Reilly?

The ghost of Shakespeare *OR* Dr. Seuss?

Triumph the Insult Comic Dog *OR* Thundarr the Barbarian?

The Deity has decided he might want to take over the world (depending on his schedule). To aid him on his quest, he's decided to make you a supervillain.

Would you rather be...

The Laminator

OR

Dr. Humidity?

Would you rather be...

Rash Man (annoys foes with minor skin irritations)

OR

The Tenderizer (softens foes with rapid strikes of a mallet)?

NOT-QUITE-SUPER-POWERS

YOU MUST CHOOSE!

Would you rather...
be able to increase the intensity/frequency of nearby throbbing objects

OR

be able to flatulate to the tune of "When the Saints Go Marching In"?

Would you rather...
have Gatorade saliva

OR

be able to murmur fluently in twelve languages?

Would you rather...

be able to insist on paying for the check but never actually get stuck with it

OR

know exactly what the person on the other end of the phone looks like simply by hearing their voice?

Would you rather...

be able to will your pot-belly to other parts of your body

OR

be first cousins with Ernest Borgnine?

Things to consider: this question excerpted from Plato's *Republic*

NOT-QUITE-SUPER-POWERS

YOU MUST CHOOSE!

(Orthodox Jews only)
Would you rather..

have nice full flowing payois

OR

always know where the matzoh is hidden?

Would you rather...

have a magic mirror that possesses Woody Allen's personality/sense of humor

OR

a coffee table that possesses the personality of ex-Pittsburgh Steeler, Franco Harris?

Would you rather...

have the power to switch your emotions on and off

OR

be able to fully comprehend written material just by sniffing the words?

Things to consider: reading in the library/on subway, leadership potential

Would you rather...

never miss throwing a quarter into a tollbooth basket

OR

defecate miniature models of famous Rodin sculptures?

NOT-QUITE-SUPER-POWERS

Good Parenting

These are the circumstances: The Deity has decided to help you rear your child. You may question his technique-- after all, he's operating for reasons beyond your understanding.

Would you rather have the entertainment at your child's birthday party be...

Tony Robbins *OR* Richard Simmons?

Charles Bukowski *OR* Jerry Falwell?

50 Cent *OR* Betty Big Ones?

YOU MUST CHOOSE!

Would you lather... (What began as a Japanese man's mispronunciation became an idea unto itself)

Would you lather... a hippopotamus?

Would you lather.... John Sununu?

Would you lather... the Fry guys?

NOT-QUITE-SUPER-POWERS

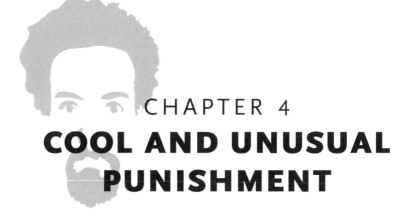

CHAPTER 4
COOL AND UNUSUAL PUNISHMENT

The Deity is in a bad mood, and deities, as you may have read, tend to be just a tad wrathful. He's looking to vent his anger on one of his pet mortals and his gaze happens to fall upon you. And so now you must suffer a horrible death, a violent torture, or something else horrific, disgusting, or just generally unpleasant.

YOU MUST CHOOSE!

Would you rather...

melon-ball your left eye out

OR

drive two spikes into your kneecaps with a sledgehammer?

Would you rather...

slide naked down a fire man's pole covered with tacks into a pool of scotch

OR

cheese-grate the skin off your left forearm?

Would you rather...

rest your head on a tee and then get smacked with the full-speed swing of Mark McGwire

OR

have a bowling ball dropped from twenty feet onto your groin?

Would you rather...

all of your drunken phone calls be recorded and played back on a popular radio station

OR

have all your love letters and emails posted on AOL's homepage?

YOU MUST CHOOSE!

Would you rather be stuck on a stalled bus with...

coked up Hollywood types *OR* obese Hare Krishnas?

incontinent Labradors *OR* the paparazzi?

forlorn albinos *OR* nosy pirates?

manic-depressive nuns *OR* autistic rodeo clowns?

condescending cobblers *OR* sullen blacksmiths ?

articulate half-orcs *OR* dizzy Erin Grey clones?

YOU MUST CHOOSE!

Would you rather have your cell phone ring function set on...

Airhorn *OR* Taser?

Throb *OR* Vacuum?

First Degree Burn *OR* Anti-Semitic Remark?

Faint *OR* Vietnam War Flashback?

Itch *OR* Ooze?

Wet Hacking Cough *OR* Surly Frenchman?

Tale of Tragic Irish Upbringing *OR* Awful Ronald Reagan Impression?

YOU MUST CHOOSE!

Would you rather...
be extruded through a spaghetti machine

OR

be buried alive in a pit of Play-Doh?

Would you rather...
dive head first off a 15 meter high-diving board into an empty pool

OR

drink a tall glass of liquid nitrogen?

Would you rather...

have your parents walk in on you while you are having sex

OR

walk in on them?

Would you rather...

chew a used condom as gum for an hour

OR

have all your pubic hairs become ingrown?

YOU MUST CHOOSE!

Would you rather...

eat every object in dictionary between "flock" and "full"

OR

between "blimp" and "brown"?

Would you rather...

roll down a hill in a barrel full of thumb tacks

OR

have a live scorpion inserted into your intestines?

Would you rather...

blend your foot and imbibe the result

OR

castrate yourself with a toe-nail clipper?

Would you rather...

be pumped with water until you burst

OR

be dehydrated to death by a giant one of those infomercial beef-jerky-making machines?

YOU MUST CHOOSE!

The Deity has imprisoned you in a closed room. You are in a fight to the death. All enemies are hostile.

Would you rather fight...

100 toddlers *OR* 15 geese?

3 possessed lawnmowers *OR* the cast of *Dawson's Creek*?

one vicious werewolf *OR* 6 bashful vampires?

extremely sleepy ninjas *OR* post-diet sumo wrestlers?

a real life incarnation of every team nickname of the NFC *OR* AFC?

a thousand evil pies *OR* a high school marching band?

Would you rather...

have your lips drawn and quartered

OR

have each of your fingers bent back until they snapped?

(For Star Trek nerds only)
Would you rather...

room with the evil Captain Kirk from Episode 27

OR

have sex with a Mugatu beast from Episode 45?

Would you rather...

have Wesley Snipes catch you picking your nose

OR

fall down in front of James Garner?

Would you rather...

as a guy, be licking a woman's breast only to discover a 3 inch hair on her nipple

OR

be kissing her lower back only to discover a tattoo of Roger Ebert?

Would you rather...

administer Tabasco sauce eye drops

OR

rub a steak knife against your gums?

Would you rather...

sleep a night on a bed of peanut butter

OR

next to a humidifier full of urine?

YOU MUST CHOOSE!

Would you rather...

take a power drill in the Adam's apple?

OR

fill your pants with raw meat and kick a pit bull in the side?

After a night of drunkenness, would you rather wake up next to...

a close co-worker *OR* a friend of your mother's?

your best friend of the opposite sex *OR* your very attractive first cousin?

the ugliest person from your high school *OR* that freaky mascot dude in the Burger King commercial?

Would you rather...

have your fingernails peeled off, one by one

OR

put your mouth around a high powered sprinkler for 15 minutes?

Would you rather...

remove your heart with a staple remover

OR

be unable to circumvent the "lather, rinse repeat" instructions on the back of shampoo bottles, perpetually shampooing yourself until starvation?

COOL AND UNUSUAL PUNISHMENT

YOU MUST CHOOSE!

Would you rather be caught masturbating by...

your grandparents *OR* your parents?

a one year old *OR* your dog?

HR Pufnstuf *OR* the ghost of Harriet Tubman?

Would you rather...

make out with someone in a dark club only to find when the lights go on that their mouth is covered in open puss-filled cold sores

OR

that it's your mother-in-law? Father-in-law? Bill Wennington?

Would you rather fight to the death...

50 remote control planes *OR* 1000 hamsters?

1000 sloths *OR* 80 penguins?

possessed office supplies *OR* possessed deli meats?

Koala bears *OR* Berenstain Bears?

25,000,000 starving ringworms *OR* the starting line-up for the New York Liberty?

Would you rather...

have your nipples gnawed off by a swarm of fire ants

OR

sit on an umbrella and then open it?

YOU MUST CHOOSE!

Would you rather...

receive a red-hot cattle prod throat culture

OR

a sulfuric acid enema?

Would you rather...

be tossed headfirst out the window 40 floors up

OR

be placed in a pit that was slowly filled with wet cement? Sand? Marbles? Lee Majors action figures?

Would you rather...

have your mom bring a blacklight into your room to reveal the various sexual fluids strewn about

OR

have to call tech support because you were surfing porn and more and more porn sites and pop-ups keep coming up on screen and so you have to talk through the problem with specifics and you're like "this website Assparade.com comes up and when I try to close it, an ad for Peter North's Volume pills comes up," and your mom comes in, and you try to close all the sites and ads real quick, like you're playing missile command on Atari, but every time you close a window, another porn ad pops open, and it's like trying to cut off the Hydra's heads, and you turn off the monitor but it's too late, and you realize that maybe it's time to move out of your parents' house?

YOU MUST CHOOSE!

Grody to the Maximum Degree:

Would you rather...

have just eaten rice only to find out they were maggots

OR

be sucking on a endless succulent strand of spaghetti only to find out it's the umbilical cord of a woman who's just given birth?

Would you rather...

stick your tongue in an electric pencil sharpener

OR

have an ant crawl up your urethra Franklin and lay hundreds of eggs?

Would you rather...

smoke 100 cigarettes nasally

OR

tongue clean 10 blocks worth of New York City public phone mouth pieces?

Would you rather...

be caught masturbating by your grandmother

OR

vice-versa?

YOU MUST CHOOSE!

Would you rather...

relax in a Jacuzzi of a stranger's saliva

OR

have diarrhea in a gravity free chamber?

Would you rather...

perform oral sex on a chronic flatulator

OR

give Forest Whitaker a handjob?

Would you rather...

find a used condom at the bottom of your vanilla latte

OR

find a dirty panty liner under the cheese in your tuna melt?

Would you rather...

watch a stripper who visibly suffers from severe arthritis *OR* who is stricken with problem flatulence?

who is 60 pounds overweight *OR* who dances with a Hitler theme?

with protruding varicose veins *OR* who eerily resembles Tommy Lasorda?

CHAPTER 5
WOULD YOU RATHER LIVE IN A WORLD WHERE...

The world is a funny place... But not funny enough. The Deity is looking to spice it up and he's hired you as a consultant. First task: come up with a better introduction to this chapter.

YOU MUST CHOOSE!

Would you rather live in a world...

where Teletubbies were a common species of creature that lived in the wild

OR

where there were evil "Bizarro" arch-enemy versions of ourselves?
Things to consider: hunting

Would you rather live in a world...

where the convention of singing "Happy Birthday" was replaced with "You Ain't Seen Nothin' Yet" by Bachman Turner Overdrive

OR

where congressional debate was settled by dodgeball contests?

Would you rather live in...

the Star Wars Universe *OR* Shakespeare's England?

a Jane Austen Novel *OR* the neighborhood with the Fat Albert gang?

Biblical Egypt *OR* the world of Atari's Centipede?

Would you rather live in...

Kaiser-ruled Germany *OR* Pre-Dorothian Oz?

Colonial Williamsburg *OR* the recreated Colonial Williamsburg?

Tsarist Russia *OR* Czarist Russia?

YOU MUST CHOOSE!

Would you rather live in a world...

where you could hit a mute button that silenced the world around you

OR

where pimps dress like mailmen and vice-versa?

Would you rather live in a world...

where there was no such thing as pain, but also no such thing as sports

OR

where there was no such thing as world hunger, but also no such thing as Jim J. Bullock?

Would you rather live in a world...

where women were given equal pay, opportunity, and access to jobs

OR

where men experience the pains of the birth process along with women?

Would you rather live in a world...

where there was a rapper-like East Coast/West Coast feud of mimes

OR

where the pledge of allegiance was changed to the lyrics to "Eye of the Tiger"?

YOU MUST CHOOSE!

Would you rather live in a world comprised entirely of...

Nerf *OR* Tootsie Roll?

flannel *OR* wicker?

ice-cream *OR* Alan Alda?

Would you rather live in a world painted by...

Van Gogh *OR* Seurat?

Rembrandt *OR* a six year old?

Monet *OR* Manet?

Bosch *OR* Boesch?

You are stranded on a desert island.

Would you rather have...

a bottle of Scope mouthwash *OR* a bottle of Jack Daniels?

a manicurist *OR* a donkey?

a slice of veal roast *OR* a poster of the 1984 Houston Rockets?

a box of Grapenuts, a wrench, and a pair of fuzzy dice *OR* a jar of Vaseline, a fake moustache, and a photograph of Spiro Agnew?

YOU MUST CHOOSE!

Would you rather live in a world without...

skin moisturizer *OR* cream cheese?

Sinbad *OR* Eskimos?

Men without Hats' "Safety Dance" *OR* salmon?

David Copperfield *OR* oatmeal?

Workin' for the Man:

The Deity has just finished a hostile take over of your work place and he's changing the place up a bit. Schooled in the art of effective management, he's seeking employee input.

Would you rather work at a company where...

you are given great health benefits

OR

Thursday is "No Pants" day?

Would you rather work at a company where...

the dress code is prom wear from the 1970's?

OR

your boss conveys your end-of-the-year evaluation through rap?

YOU MUST CHOOSE!

Would you rather be...

a crash test dummy *OR* a fluffer for animal nature documentaries?
the world's greatest rhythm gymnast *OR* the last man off the bench for the LA Clippers?
a Lionel Richie impersonator *OR* a Hobbit pimp?
a matador with a club foot *OR* a librarian with problem flatulence?
Or the reverse?

Would you rather be...

a human mannequin that just stands there all day and models clothes in a department store

OR

a ruthless and slick Special Olympics sports agent?

Would you rather...

have your therapist be James Taylor OR Bob Costas?

have your Lamaze coach be Marv Albert OR the guy from *Police Academy* who made all those crazy sound effects?

your minister be Gallagher OR Andrew "Dice" clay?

your blacksmith be Dan Rather OR John Stamos?

WOULD YOU RATHER LIVE IN A WORLD WHERE...

YOU MUST CHOOSE!

Would you rather.... for beginners:

Would you rather...

be suave and sophisticated with nice hair
OR
rotund and misshapen with rickets?

Would you rather...

learn the teachings of Jesus
OR
those of Timothy Busfield?

YOU MUST CHOOSE!

The Would You Rather...? Menu

Would you rather eat...

200 slices of American cheese OR 2000 raisins?

a cube of dry ice OR your own left foot?

the contents of a full vacuum cleaner bag OR forty-five dollars in nickels?

Would you rather eat...

a bowl of bat guano OR a mug of hot tea prepared with a used tampon?

14 full sticks of butter OR the contents of Michael Jackson's face?

all food in liquid form OR gaseous form?

Baked penguin OR Creamed Estrada?

WOULD YOU RATHER LIVE IN A WORLD WHERE...

YOU MUST CHOOSE!

Would you rather drink...

a **Beefbrawler** (gin, orange juice, ground beef, two shakers of salt sucked through a green onion)

OR

a **Bloody Pilgrim** (Kool-Aid, heavy cream and mushrooms pureed, topped with warm fat freshly liposucked from Elizabeth Taylor's thigh and upper arm)?

Would you rather eat...

The Emperor (2 pounds of roast beef sautéed in Roger Ebert's sweat consumed to the tune of "Ride of the Valkyrie")?

OR

The Regent (2 charcoal briquettes on a toasted roll, eaten in the presence of 5 surly sailors)?

CHAPTER 6
WISHFUL THINKING

The Deity has assumed corporeal form. He wears a white suit, and is flanked by a miniature Latino man, also wearing a white suit. A plane is heard overhead, exciting the small man to announce its arrival. Twice. This could mean only one thing. You have arrived on Fantasy Island. Not only do you have the chance to fulfill a fantasy, but you get to choose between two.

YOU MUST CHOOSE!

Would you rather...

have a lake named after you

OR

have a popular children's multivitamin shaped in your image?

Would you rather interview...

Bill Clinton *OR* Prince?

Dick Gephart *OR* Dominique Wilkins?

J.D. Salinger *OR* J.D. Hogg

Jesus *OR* Tom Kite?

If you could go back in time, would you rather...

dance with Fred Astaire *OR* be serenaded by Frank Sinatra?

have Leonardo DaVinci paint your portrait *OR* have Shakespeare write you a sonnet?

have Mozart compose a symphony for you *OR* have Jeff Foxworthy compose a "You Might Be A Redneck If..." joke in your honor?

Would you rather...

get drunk-dialed by Gandhi

OR

by Martin Luther King?

WISHFUL THINKING

YOU MUST CHOOSE!

Would you rather...
bring in da' noise
OR
bring in da' funk?

Would you rather see...
Barry White chant the haftorah portion at a Bar-Mitzvah
OR
Al Gore do def comedy?

Would you rather have sex with...

Batman *OR* Super Man?

The Flash *OR* Spiderman?

Toucan Sam *OR* Cap'n Crunch?

Things to consider: Cap'n Crunch's penchant for buggery

Would you rather have sex with...

The Bionic Woman *OR* Wilma from *Buck Rogers*?

Wonder Woman *OR* a real-life anatomically correct Barbie?

Snow White *OR* Rapunzel?

Things to consider: likely Rapunzel winterbush

WISHFUL THINKING

YOU MUST CHOOSE!

Would you rather...
be on a reality show

OR

punch everyone who has been?

Would you rather...
see Lincoln and Washington debate

OR

see them play a game of one-on-one basketball?

Would you rather...

touch the Pope

OR

meet Bill Bellamy?

Would you rather...

have a mountain range named after you

OR

have a sexual position officially named after you?

WISHFUL THINKING

YOU MUST CHOOSE!

Would you rather spend a day with...

El DeBarge *OR* George Bernard Shaw?

Ralph Sampson *OR* Ralph Nader?

Rommel and Charles Schultz *OR* Willie Nelson and Kubla Khan?

The founding fathers *OR* the cast of *The Cannonball Run 1* and *2*?

If you could were a fly on the wall, would you rather reside...

on Tom Cruise's wall *OR* on Robin Williams's?

on porn queen Jenna Jameson's wall *OR* on Dungeons and Dragons creator Gary Gygax's?

on Tone Loc's wall *OR* Anne Maxson's?

Would you rather have sex with...

just the top half of Briana Banks *OR* just the bottom half of Britney Spears?

a Filipino Justin Timberlake *OR* an Caucasian Samuel L. Jackson?

Clint Howard *OR* Kate Beckinsale, 10 seconds after she passed away?

Topher Grace *OR* Kevin James? If they exchanged weights?

Valerie Bertinelli with a glass eye *OR* Agatha Christie with 42DD breasts?

Would you rather split a bottle of whiskey with...

Jimmy "Super Fly" Snuka *OR* Andy Rooney?

Wilfred Brimley *OR* Webster?

Hunter S. Thompson *OR* Manute Bol?

WISHFUL THINKING

YOU MUST CHOOSE!

Would you rather...

have sex with Paris Hilton

OR

punch her in the face?

Would you rather...

play Electronic Battleship with Tyra Banks

OR

help Michelle Kwan assemble a bookshelf?

Would you rather...

lasso Gabe Kaplan

OR

set up a volleyball net for Helen Hunt?

(Dr. Seuss fans only)
Would you rather have sex with...

Salma Hayek on a kayak

OR

Halle Berry on a ferry? Penelope Cruz in grey ooze?

YOU MUST CHOOSE!

The Deity encourages adventure in the bedroom between two consenting adults. You and your significant other are to participate in a role-playing fantasy...

Would you rather fantasize the scenario of...

"Rugged Cowboy Discovers Handmaiden in the Barn" *OR* "Cheerleader Approaches Bookish Professor After Class"?

"Secretary and Boss Working Late" *OR* "Tax Session with Accountant Ignites Passions"?

"Fan Meets Post-Concert Fabio" *OR* "Cashier Bumps Into Anonymous Thin Moroccan In Arby's Bathroom Stall"?

Would you rather...

have sex with a woman with Kathy Bates's body on the top half and Carmen Electra's body on the bottom half

OR

Carmen Electra's on top and Kathy Bates's body on the bottom?

Would you rather...

have sex with Harrison Ford *OR* Han Solo?

Sean Penn *OR* Jeff Spicoli?

Hugh Jackman *OR* Wolverine?

Jeff Bridges *OR* Starman and The Dude (Jeff Lebowski) together?

Angelina Jolie *OR* Lara Croft?

Douglas Rain *OR* Hal9000?

WISHFUL THINKING

WOULD YOU RATHER...?

YOU MUST CHOOSE!

Intermission: Spell-check Highlights

Sometimes Microsoft Word's spell-check can be a life-saver. Other times...

Word not in dictionary	-	Spell-check's suggestion
Chewbacca	-	chewable
Fartbeat	-	ferryboat
Beefball	-	befall
Buttball	-	butyl, biteable
Fillmore	-	filmier, filmgoer
briss	-	RBI's
McCheese	-	machete
dickwad	-	duckweed
Yankovic	-	no suggestions

The names of various famous people that have appeared in drafts of this book have been replaced with the spell-check's suggestions. Try to figure out the actual names. Answers on page 240

Suggested words- famous person

1. Cyanide Pauper - ?

2. Simian Believer - ?

3. Fabliau, phobia, FBI - ? (clue: Italian superhunk)

4. Jason Boatmen - ?

5. Lays Milan - ?

6. Elite Gourd - ?

7. Cedar, Pig - ?

WISHFUL THINKING

CHAPTER 7
PLAY BALL!

Professional sports are in trouble. Free agency has obliterated team loyalty, good sportsmanship is a thing of the past, and the game is so much about the dollar that rotisserie leagues now have fans fantasizing they are owners, competing with each other to make the most money. Something needs to be done about the sorry state of sports. Enter the Deity (and you.)

YOU MUST CHOOSE!

You have just been hired by the head of the PGA to change one rule.

Would you rather...

allow loud heckling at greens

OR

require golfers to tee off of their caddy's crotch?

Would you rather...

fill bunkers with thousands of fire ants

OR

quicksand?

You have just been chosen to help pick one rule to make soccer more exciting.

Would you rather...

have grazing livestock scattered throughout the field

OR

if a goal is not scored in a game, have all players summarily executed?

Would you rather...

replace the grass with poison oak

OR

make players play in high heels?

PLAY BALL!

YOU MUST CHOOSE!

As NBA commissioner,

Would you rather institute...
a 2 second shot clock

OR

a 3 feet tall maximum height rule?

Would you rather...
cover the court in Teflon

OR

require that trash-talking be in Old English?

WOULD YOU RATHER...?

YOU MUST CHOOSE!

You have been appointed baseball commissioner.

Would you rather...

put spikes on the outfield wall at baseball games

OR

light the bases on fire?

Would you rather...

if a player balks, he is shot on sight

OR

if a fan catches a foul ball, that fan gets to "do it" with that player's wife?

Things to consider: That last joke might be from old Letterman. We can't even remember.

PLAY BALL!

WOULD YOU RATHER...?   125

You have just become boxing commissioner.

Would you rather...

limit punching to below the belt

OR

require whoopie cushion-like devices to be placed in gloves?

Would you rather...

have tag-team matches

OR

have a round where boxers dance-off?

Mixed Blessings

"You take the good, you take the bad, you take them both and there you have the facts of life, the facts of life..." – Walt Whitman

Would you rather...

be able to jump like Dr. J. in the ABA but always have to wear those short shorts he had

OR

have the eloquence of Thomas Jefferson but have to wear colonial garb and wig?

Would you rather...

be incredibly charming, but only when discussing your bowel movements

OR

have an infallible pick-up line, but only with Fuddruckers employees?

PLAY BALL!

YOU MUST CHOOSE!

Would you rather...

have the mind of William Shakespeare but the body of William Taft

OR

the mind of Albert Einstein but the body of Fat Albert?

Things to Consider: Possible "Fat Einstein" Cartoon

Would you rather...

be found attractive by all members of the opposite sex, but secrete copious amounts of steak sauce when aroused

OR

have genitals that permanently tasted like chocolate, but have all your offspring be exact clones of Walter Matthau?

Would you rather...

be a brilliant essayist but have to wear a matching set of wristbands and headband at all times

OR

have heightened Stratego intuition, but talk like Liberace when asked to repeat yourself?

Would you rather...

look respectable in sweat pants but articulate all your thoughts aloud

OR

have a great short game in golf, but compulsively fondle yourself when the doorbell rings?

Things to consider: cocktail parties, making business deals

YOU MUST CHOOSE!

Would you rather...

have the courage of a lion but the ass of a baboon

OR

the wisdom of an owl but the head of Epstein from *Welcome Back, Kotter?*

Would you rather...

have a firm handshake but be severely lactose intolerant

OR

be loved by animals but require the signature of Cheech Marin for all your legal documents?

Would you rather...

have a knack for model train set-ups but have an irresistible urge to punch people named Mildred in the breast and thighs

OR

be able to make anything shiny but be unable to refrain from making the tug boat gesture and sound any time an overweight person enters a room?

Would you rather...

be an awesome winker but have ear lobes that melt like candle wax when it gets hot

OR

be able to exactly gauge the amount of cream and sugar in your coffee instinctually but have to always wear a fruit roll-up yarmulke?

PLAY BALL!

YOU MUST CHOOSE!

Would you rather...

be implanted with the love child of Adam Ant and Aunt Jemima

OR

Woody Allen and Ray Allen?

Things to consider: this question came to Gomberg in a dream

Would you rather...

have a 3 constitution and a 15 charisma

OR

an 18 constitution and a 10 charisma?

Things to consider: this question came to Gomberg in a nightmare

CHAPTER 8
MORE SEX

The Deity just can't get enough. Enough of meddling with your sex life, that is. Exactly what he is compensating for is unclear, though it must be quite a significant deficiency judging from the wrath-level evident in these debauched dilemmas.

YOU MUST CHOOSE!

Would you rather...

during sex, be able to read the mind of the person you are having sex with

OR

be able to hit your or your partner's g-spot by finding Waldo in a *Where's Waldo* book? (each page can be used once)

Would you rather...

acquire all the knowledge of people you have sex with

OR

right before you climax, have the choice to store up orgasms to experience later, like the "downloading later" function on email?

Things to consider: rainy days, orgasm breaks at work, nerd-banging

Would you rather...

have your genitalia located on the palm of your left hand *OR* the front of your neck?

on the middle of your back *OR* on your elbow?

on your hip *OR* your ankle?

Things to consider: oral sex, masturbation, tailoring bills

Would you rather...

have breast implants made of Nerf *OR* Play-doh?

quarters *OR* thumb tacks?

coffee grounds *OR* Pillsbury Doughboys?

tadpoles *OR* helium?

Things to consider: babies' high-pitched cries after breast-feeding

MORE SEX

YOU MUST CHOOSE!

Would you rather...

have a penis that sheds skin like a snake every week
OR
a penis that makes the sound of a rainstick when it moves?

Would you rather...

have to use condoms two times too big *OR* two times too small?

aluminum foil condoms *OR* the same condom over and over?

condoms covered in sandpaper *OR* condoms covered with pictures
of your mother?

Would you rather...

have a neurological abnormality that causes you to appeal victoriously to an imaginary crowd à la Hulk Hogan after sex

OR

have a condition where as soon as you see someone take their clothes off, you point to the "appropriate" body parts and say quite suavely, "milk, milk, lemonade, 'round the corner fudge is made"?

Would you rather...

every hour on the hour, change which gender you are attracted to

OR

turn your sexual partner into Tony Danza when you climax, and then turn them back to themselves the next time you have sex with them?
Things to consider: maintaining a marriage, determining who the boss is

---

YOU MUST CHOOSE!

Would you rather...

utter all exclamations during sex in Yiddish *OR* Chinese?

in sign language *OR* in the form of a question as if on *Jeopardy*?

in Pig Latin *OR* with IM acronyms?

Things to consider: rabgay hattay itttaytay; lol, brb, ftp, diithbh, ccr, elo, bto

Would you rather...

ejaculate a deadly dart

OR

die if you are not having sex at 3:37 pm every day?

Things to consider: moving to Vegas, pulling out, work as a spy

YOU MUST CHOOSE!

Would you rather...

have dreadlocked pubes

OR

have nipple-itis (constant visibly erect nipples that show through anything you wear)?

Things to considers: tuxedoes, the beach, short shorts

Would you rather...

have a scrotum that fills with fresh-popped popcorn upon getting aroused (à la Jiffy Pop)

OR

make the sound of a foghorn upon orgasm?

MORE SEX

WOULD YOU RATHER...?

Would you rather have sex with...

Chelsea Clinton *OR* a jaundiced Sandra Bullock?

an albino Freddie Prinze, Jr. *OR* a severely sun-burnt Matt LeBlanc?

a 400 pound person on top *OR* a 300 pound person on crack?

a Chinese version of Courtney Cox *OR* a black version of Reese Witherspoon?

WWE's Chyna *OR* Mandy Moore if she was missing an arm? Both arms? And a leg? Just a torso and a head?

Would you rather...

have pornographic pop-up ads constantly appearing in your thoughts

OR

have your cell phone wired into your body with the ring function set on "orgasm"?

Would you rather live in a world where...

corporate hold music was phone sex

OR

Casual Friday was preceded by Thong Thursday?

YOU MUST CHOOSE!

Would you rather...

lactate spider webbing *OR* dental floss?

Milwaukee's Best *OR* spray paint?

holy water *OR* penicillin?

Would you rather...

watch Girls Gone Wild
OR
Rabbis Gone Wild?

Would you rather have a threesome with...

Karl Rove and Sally Struthers *OR* Carrot Top and Margaret Thatcher?

Kate Hudson and Rey Mysterio, Jr *OR* Ed Bradley and Amber Lynn?

Wolf Blitzer and Liv Tyler *OR* your significant other and Arnold Palmer's caddie?

Would you rather...

have your entire sexual history be re-enacted by the animatronic robots in a Disney World ride á la the *Pirates of the Caribbean*?

OR

have the moments and characters in your sex life released by the Franklin Mint as a series of collectible porcelain figurines?

YOU MUST CHOOSE!

Would you rather have...

9 inch nipples *OR* a 9 inch clitoris?

a 24 month menstrual cycle *OR* a 24 hour menstrual cycle?

a 4 pound tongue *OR* a 4 pound testicle?

Would you rather have sex with...

Maroon 5 *OR* Blink 182

Sum 51 *OR* Matchbox 20

Front 242 *OR* Florp 968?

Would you rather...

have your mom have to put on your condoms like she was dressing you as a child for the winter

OR

never be able to call your spouse by the same name twice?

Things to consider: coming up with new terms of endearment – Honey, Baby, Schnookeylups, Porko, Flartran, Sweetballs, Fatooshk

Would you rather your pimp be...

Strom Thurmond *OR* Emmanuel Lewis?

Grimace *OR* Chewbacca?

Vijay Singh *OR* Beetle Bailey?

YOU MUST CHOOSE!

Pick Your Scrotum!

Would you rather have...

a scrotum slightly too small for your testicles *OR* a scrotum that was 40 times bigger than it is currently? (testicles remain the same size)

a transparent scrotum *OR* a denim scrotum?

a plaid scrotum *OR* a bungie-scrotum™

Things to consider: other books that have an entire page dedicated to the scrotum: James Joyce's *Ulysses*, *Where's Waldo?*, the *Bible*, Jane Austen's *Scrotum*

Would you...

perform oral sex on (insert undesirable acquaintance) to have sex with (insert celebrity)?

Would you rather...

tag on the phrase "for a girl" to every compliment you give a female

OR

tag on a sarcastic "Sherlock" to every sexual exclamation you utter?

Would you rather live in a world where...

condoms were able to magically crawl out of the wrapper and put themselves on at exactly the right moment

OR

there was a male contraceptive pill that caused some bloating and moodiness?

YOU MUST CHOOSE!

Date, Marry, or Screw?

Here's an oldie but a goodie. We give you three names. You decide which one you'd marry, which you'd date, and which you'd screw.

Bill Clinton, George Bush, George Bush Sr.

Alec Baldwin, Stephen Baldwin, Daniel Baldwin

Michael Jackson circa Thriller, Michael Jackson circa Bad, Michael Jackson now

Britney Spears, Jessica Simpson, Mariah Carey

Condoleezza Rice, Connie Chung, the hot Hooters waitress with low self esteem

Date, Marry, Screw, Play Ping Pong Against, or Create a Revolutionary Movement With?

Okay, you mastered that one. Now to challenge you, we've added a few more options and names, resulting in more permutations. Here you must decide, which name you'd marry, which you'd date, which you'd screw, which you'd play ping-pong against, and which you would start a revolutionary movement with.

Ben Affleck, Matt Damon, Che Guevara, ping pong champion John Hu, Mel Gibson

Tommy Lee, Ben Franklin, Tim Duncan, The Rock, Alan Greenspan

Courtney Cox, Lisa Kudrow, Jennifer Aniston, Deborah Messing, your mother

Al Sharpton, Corey Feldman, Corey Haim, Venus Williams, the girl at Starbucks who looks a little like Larry Bird

---

YOU MUST CHOOSE!

Pretty good, but can you handle this one?

Date, Marry, Screw, Discuss the War of 1812 with, Accompany to Six Flags Amusement Park, or Collaborate to Write Hip Hop Album?

Jerome Bettis, Molly Ringwald, George Stephanopoulos, Eminem, Menudo, God

UN Ambassador John Boland, 50 Cent, Tiger Woods, The Teletubbies, Patrick Swayze, Roberto Benigni

Maria Shriver, Bill Wennington, Darth Maul, Hitler, a can of tennis balls, Gomberg

Would you rather use as sex toys...

a tetherball, a map of Uruguay, and a menorah

OR

some measuring spoons, a thermos, and a Mark Eaton rookie card?

You live with a roommate. You decide to use a blacklight to check your room for hidden "stains."

Would you rather find stains all over...

your washcloth *OR* your favorite cereal bowl?

your computer keyboard and mouse *OR* a framed photo of your family?

a copy of George Washington Carter's autobiography *OR* a copy of *Would You Rather...?: Ultimate Challenge*?

YOU MUST CHOOSE!

Would you rather...

have testicles with the density of hydrogen

OR

prematurely ejaculate by two weeks?

Would you rather..

think about sex every 6 or 7 seconds

OR

think about Chinese rice farmers tilling their fields every 6 or 7 seconds?
Things to consider: which is more arousing?

YOU MUST CHOOSE!

Would you rather...

turn into Rip Taylor when masturbating

OR

have your sexual appetite vary directly with your proximity to Radio Shack?

Would you rather...

have to use condoms that come in a wrapper where you have to finish the crossword puzzle before it can be opened

OR

be unable to shake the image of Meadowlark Lemon during all sexual congress?

YOU MUST CHOOSE!

Would you rather have breast implants made of...

attracting magnets *OR* repelling magnets?

locusts *OR* throbbing hearts?

brie cheese *OR* the spirit of Malcolm X?

Would you rather...

have troll doll heads for nipples

OR

pipe cleaners for pubic hair?

Would you rather have sex with...

The Tin Man *OR* The Scarecrow?

Mr. Belvedere *OR* Matlock?

your dentist *OR* your 3rd grade PE teacher?

the "Where's the Beef" lady *OR* the "I've fallen and I can't get up!" lady?

Skeletor *OR* Gargamel?

YOU MUST CHOOSE!

Would you rather...

be bisexually attracted to men and fish

OR

tri-sexually attracted to men, women, and boxes of Milk Duds?

Would you rather...

be required to file an official request with the federal government in order to receive oral sex

OR

have "Total number of sexual partners" be a required box to fill out on every job application?

Would you rather...

have sex with a guy who has the body of John Goodman and the face of Brad Pitt

OR

the body of Brad Pitt and the face of Mayor McCheese?

Would you rather...

have sex with a woman that has the body of Janet Reno and the face of Angelina Jolie

OR

the body of Angelina Jolie and the face of former Milwaukee Buck Jack Sikma?

Things to consider: doggie-style

YOU MUST CHOOSE!

Would you rather have phone sex with...

Dr. Laura Schlessinger *OR* Martha Stewart?

Barbara Bush *OR* Hillary Clinton?
Things to consider: Barbara Bush has a mouth like a sailor

Barbara Streisand *OR* the ghost of Harriet Tubman?

someone who constantly corrects your grammar *OR* someone
prone to quoting Joseph Goebbels throughout?

Gary Gnu *OR* Pegasus?

The Deity, though known to have assumed corporeal form to rape mortals and livestock, is a believer in safe sex for you. Sort of...

Would you rather your only means of birth control be...

gum *OR* an English muffin?

a rubber band and a box of tic-tacs *OR* a roll of "Jazz Icon" postage stamps?

a waffle cone *OR* anal sex?

a stapler *OR* an 8"x10" photograph of Wilfred Brimley?

MORE SEX

YOU MUST CHOOSE!

Would you rather...

have sex with Tom Brady and get herpes

OR

have sex with Tim Russert and get a sensible but stylish tote bag?

Would you rather...

have sex with Jenna Jameson and get crabs

OR

have sex with Katie Couric and get a nice pair of business-casual wrinkle-free slacks with solid craftsmanship?

Would you rather...

never be able to experience orgasm

OR

perpetually experience orgasm?

Things to consider: life at the office, bar-mitzvahs, special pants, porn career

Would you rather have a vagina...

that acts as a guillotine 1 out of every 8 times an object is inserted *OR* one that secretes sulfuric acid upon orgasm?

that doubles as a trash compactor *OR* a cassette player?

that howls like a wolf when the moon is full *OR* one that belts out the lyrics to Sinatra tunes on command?

MORE SEX

YOU MUST CHOOSE!

Ménage a Troiseses

Would you rather have a three-way with...

Flavor Flav and Teri Hatcher *OR* Ted Koppel and Kelly Ripa?

Jennifer Connelly and Lawrence Taylor *OR* Jennifer Garner and Nelson Mandela?

the Olsen twins *OR* the Wonder Twins?

the Guinness Book of Records World's Fattest Twins (the ones who are always shown on motorcycles) *OR* the Guinness Book of Records World's Tallest Man and World's Shortest Man?

Things to consider: Note to self: Idea for TV show: The fat twins on motorcycles become motorcycle cops; also: try to make sentence with as many colons as possible.

Would you rather...

get punched hard in the gut by the person on your left
OR
kissed passionately by the person on your right?

Would you rather have sex with...

a 5'2" version of Ashton Kutcher *OR* Jason Bateman if he put on 50 pounds?

a soft and tender Don Cheadle *OR* an excitingly rough Kermit the Frog?

Antonio Banderas without limbs *OR* Tobey Maguire with an extra one?

a chain smoking Kofi Annan *OR* Ben Kingsley playing kazoo?

Pornification

By Andrew Ackerman

Pornographers are quick to capitalize on the success of mainstream movies. All it takes to turn an actual movie into a pornographic film is a slight tweak of the title. This process is called "Pornification."

For example,

Good Will Hunting, when pornified, becomes Good Will Humping

Similarly, *The Terminator* becomes, of course, The Sperminator

For every legit movie, there exists (at least theoretically) a porn version of that movie.

Test your understanding of Pornification on the next two pages with our Pornification Quiz.

Pornification (continued)

Here are some pornified titles. Can you figure out the original Hollywood film that inspired them? Answers on page 241.

1. American Booty

2. Titty Lickers

3. Grinding Nemo

Now, the fun part. We give you the popular movie title. Can you pornify it? Answers on page 241.

4. The Nutty Professor

5. S.W.A.T.

6. Toy Story

MORE SEX

YOU MUST CHOOSE!

Pornification (continued)

More titles to pornify.

7. Big Trouble in Little China

8. Analyze This

9. Glory

10. Space Jam

11. Malcolm X

12. Chitty Chitty Bang Bang

13. Shaft

14. Cold Mountain

15. Lou Dobbs Moneyline

Sins

Choose the lesser of two evils.

Would you rather...

burn down an orphanage

OR

run over a litter of kittens with your lawn mower?

Would you rather...

kick your aunt in the stomach

OR

drop 200 turtles off a 40 story building?

Immoral Dilemmas

- You are walking down the street and see an open briefcase with $1,000 in it. Across the street there is a police station. Do you spend the money on whores or crack?

- Your boss, female, attractive, and married has insinuated that pleasuring her sexually will result in the advancement of your career. Do you partake in oral or anal sex?

- You're driving at night and hit a dog. No one witnesses you hitting the dog. Do you broil or bake it?

- You're waiting at a red light at 4 AM. There isn't a car in sight. No one would see if you ran the light. Do you masturbate with your left or right hand?

- An old dirty vagrant with lip sores is pulled from the water and needs mouth-to-mouth resuscitation, which you know how to do. Do you partake in oral or anal sex?

CHAPTER 9
WOULD YOU...

The Deity, in addition to being vengeful and sadistic, is lazy. So lazy in fact that he didn't even bother to finish his catchphrase. The result is the more abbreviated but just as puzzling "Would You..?"

YOU MUST CHOOSE!

Would you... punch your grandmother, not full-force, but solidly in the back of the neck for $16,500?

Would you... have sex with John Daly daily, to have sex with Keira Knightly, nightly?

Would you... want to be immune from all traffic laws if you had to drive a '70's style van with a moonscape and Pegasus airbrushed on the side?

Would you... share an apartment with Corey Feldman to lower your rent by $600 a month?

Would you... have sex with someone who had a perfect body of the opposite sex but has your face?

Would you... permanently chain a penguin to your leg to be able to have sex with anyone you want?

Would you... wear your hair in a mullet for a month for $1200? (for women, $3900?)

Would you... cuddle with Boris Yeltzin to get your own sitcom with Justine Bateman? Vice-Versa?

(for men) **Would you...** dance with a woman if you knew it would never lead to sex?

Would you... dedicate a book to your mothers if the book was full of vile, infantile and prurient material including the phrase "wagon-trained by a quartet of sex-starved Ewoks"?

WOULD YOU...

YOU MUST CHOOSE!

"The Million Dollar Man" Ted Dibiase once said that every man has his price, and the Deity's about to find out yours. He's making you an offer you can't refuse...or can you? If you can refuse the offer, name your price.

Would you... eat a tennis ball for $1,000?

Would you... spend two weeks in nothing but a g-string for $2,000?

Would you... sleep with your significant other's best friend for $10,000? What if that significant other was "Handsome" Harley Race?

Would you... gain 150 pounds for $10,000?

Would you... (if male) give up an inch of your height for an inch of penis size? If female, would you trade one inch of your significant other's height for an inch added to his penis size? How many inches would you trade?

Would you... run full speed into a brick wall for a life-size wax sculpture of Nipsey Russell?

Would you... give up socks if France promised to change its name to Funkytown?

YOU MUST CHOOSE!

Would you... like to be a member of the Libertarian party?

Would you... compliment Jimmy Carter's presidency for an egg sandwich and medium coffee?

Would you... want the artistic talents of Picasso if you could only paint guys named Cyrus?

Would you... have sex with a 70 year old Marlon Brando to have sex with a 30 year old Marlon Brando?

Would you... have sex with a walrus to have sex with all the Playmates of the current year (men); with People's 50 Sexiest Men (women)?

Would you... make out with and grope feverishly your best friend's mom for forty minutes for $15,000?

Would you... want a second portable set of "voo-doo doll" genitalia that communicates all sensation to your real genitalia? Things to consider: theft, pets, surreptitious self-pleasure

Would you... submerge your balls in boiling water for 10 seconds to have a 10 second glimpse of creation?

Would you... dry-hump Neal Patrick Harris for a complete understanding of badminton strategy?

WOULD YOU...

YOU MUST CHOOSE!

Would you... spend two weeks wearing nothing but a g-string and Tevas for $2,000?

Would you... give up 2 years of your life to have a penis that was 3 inches longer (men) or breasts that were 3 sizes larger (women)?

Would you... take the surname of your spouse upon marriage if it were "Vulvatron?"

Would you... as a man, get breast implants for $100,000? (They can be removed after a year.)

Let's get right to the point. **Would you** bang the Michelin Man for a 64 inch flat screen plasma TV?

Would you... let a stranger have sex with your spouse for $100,000 dollars? $500,000? $2,000,000? What if that stranger was former NBA great Ralph Sampson?

Would you... bludgeon thirty baby seals to death to have sex with Penelope Cruz? Vice-versa?

Would you... butter Eric Montross to be impervious to tan lines?

Would you... want to be able to perform oral sex on yourself?
Things to consider: never wanting to leave the house, which leads to lack of exercise, which leads to weight gain, which leads to no longer being able to continue said ability

Be hole-punched to death

OR

Be eaten alive by the cast of Diff'rent Strokes?

WOULD YOU....

WOULD YOU...

Would you rather...

Have the head of Herve Villechaize (Fantasy Island's Tattoo) in place of your left hand and the head of Ricardo Montalban (Fantasy Island's Mr. Rourke) in place of your right hand

OR

be unable to go places without an entourage of bickering Vietnamese politicians?

©Justin Heimberg &David Gomberg Wouldyourather.com

CHAPTER 10
DATING AND MARRIAGE

Dating and marriage, much like the workings of the Deity, often seem to unfold according to reasons beyond our understanding. Consequently, the Deity feels you could use a little direction when it comes to such matters. Of course, always a believer in free will, he allows you the ultimate choice.

Would you rather...

marry the spouse of your dreams but gain 10 pounds a year
OR
have them gain 10 pounds a year?

Would you rather...

have a lover who is 6'3 tall with a 3 inch penis *OR* 5'2 tall with a 9 inch penis?

7' tall with a 1 inch penis *OR* 2' tall with a 12 inch penis?

18' tall with a 4 inch penis *OR* 1' tall with a 64 inch penis?

Would you rather...

date someone with a razor sharp wit

OR

a vibrating tongue?

Would you rather...

only be able to pick up guys/chicks via middle school style notes folded with hearts

OR

by window-side serenades of hits from the early '80s?

Things to consider: creative I-dotting, *Total Eclipse of the Heart*, *All Out of Love*, *Turning Japanese*, *Rocket*

YOU MUST CHOOSE!

Would you rather...

date someone with a winterbush (very heavy unkempt pubic hair)
OR
an autumnbush (hair changes color and falls out in fall)?

Would you rather...

marry someone whose desired personal space was 2 inches
OR
30 feet?

Would you rather...

your Lamaze coach be that excitable Spanish soccer announcer

OR

Jesse Jackson?

Would you rather...

your marriage counselor be Dr. Drew

OR

Dr. Dre?

DATING AND MARRIAGE

YOU MUST CHOOSE!

Would you rather have your love life written by...

Ally McBeal creator David E. Kelly *OR* porn czar Seymore Butts?

Woody Allen *OR* Nicholas Sparks?

Charles Bukowski *OR* Sir Mix-A-lot?

Things to consider: honesty pertaining to advocating of large posterior, tendency of other brothers to fabricate

Would you rather marry...

an ugly rock star *OR* a hot garbage man?

a rich, shallow investment banker *OR* a poor, brilliant artist?

a self-righteous milkman *OR* a melancholy locksmith?

a bipolar tour guide *OR* an autistic Foot Locker salesperson?

Would you rather...

have your wedding conducted in the tone of a rap video

OR

in the tone of an elementary school play?

DATING AND MARRIAGE

YOU MUST CHOOSE!

Would you rather...

date someone who only wants to have sex once a month

OR

date someone who made you solve a riddle before moving to each new step sexually?

Things to consider: what is the angle between the hands of a clock if the clock shows 3:15? If you answered, "7.5 degrees," you may now fondle my breasts.

Would you rather be proposed to...

in the New York Times crossword puzzle *OR* with skywriting?

in a robot imitation *OR* written backwards in blood on the wall?

on the Jumbotron screen at a baseball game *OR* be divorced on the Jumbotron screen at a baseball game?

Would you rather...

spend your honeymoon in a Home Depot *OR* a bowling alley?

in a slaughterhouse *OR* at your mom's house?

at a four day Civil War re-enactment *OR* at a Vietnam War re-enactment?

For your wedding, would you rather...

be registered at Quiznos *OR* at the Chuck E. Cheese prize counter?

an S&M shop *OR* a D&D shop?

Leo's House of Gauze *OR* All Things Tungsten?

DATING AND MARRIAGE

YOU MUST CHOOSE!

Would you rather date...

a woman who loves to give oral sex, but while doing it, hums the tune to the *Sanford and Son* theme song

OR

a woman who talks filthy but speaks in the voice of Yosemite Sam?

Would you rather date...

a woman with a great body but simple conversations skills

OR

a woman who speaks with wit and insight but keeps her hand perpetually soaking in a bowl of wet spinach?

Would you rather...

draw your dating pool from people browsing the Self Help section of the book store

OR

the Sci-Fi section?

Would you rather...

when you get a prospective date's number or e-mail, only be able to write it down by tattooing it on your body

OR

your only pick-up line be: "To answer your question – Yes. Light weights, high reps."?

YOU MUST CHOOSE!

The deity has released a line of new colognes.

Would you rather wear...

New Tennis Ball *OR*   Wet German Shepherd?

Mulch *OR* Pungent Reefer ?

Eau de Gomberg *OR* Eau de Heimberg?

Would you rather date...

a prop comedian *OR* a compulsive air guitarist?

a half-woman/half horse *OR* a half-woman/half-couch?

someone with an inverse farmer's tan *OR* someone who smells their fingers every ten seconds?

On a first date with someone you really like, would you rather...

be unable to talk about anything other than the mechanism that causes grass stains

OR

have to use the phrase "white power" 20 times?

Would you rather...

have your wedding vows written by gangsta rappers

OR

by the author of one of those African spam money request emails?

Things to consider: "It is of the utmost Urgency with which I submit this plea for your sincerest Love and Trustworthiness?"

DATING AND MARRIAGE

YOU MUST CHOOSE!

For your wedding, would you rather...

have a paintball war at the reception

OR

enter down the aisle to the tune of "We're Not Gonna Take It" by Twisted Sister?

Would you rather...

have a "save game" function on a date

OR

a pause function?

This Or That? Answers are on page 240.

Challenge yourself or your friends with the following quiz.

1. Supreme Court Justice or Venereal Disease?
   a. Scalia

   b. Gonorrhea

   c. Chlamydia

   d. Bader Ginsburg

2. Bible Chapter or Porn Magazine?
   a. Revelation

   b. Cheri

   c. Genesis

   d. Barely Legal

DATING AND MARRIAGE

This Or That? (con't)

3. Batman Villain or Dildo?
   a. The Penguin

   b. The Emperor

   c. The Joker

   d. The Tickler

4. Catskills Comedian or VD Symptom?
   a. Clammy Hands

   b. Shecky Green

   c. Swollen Glands

   d. Soupy Sales

CHAPTER 11
GETTING PERSONAL

It's your turn to play Deity. Challenge your friends with these personalizable dilemmas.

YOU MUST CHOOSE!

Would you rather...

play strip poker with (insert three relatives)

OR

rub oil on every inch of (insert vile acquaintance)?

Would you rather...

call up (insert set of friend's parents), state your name, and have phone sex

OR

take a shower with (insert somebody else's parents)?

Would you rather...

be caught masturbating by (insert friend of the family)

OR

catch (insert friend of the family) masturbating?

Would you rather...

have oral sex with (insert unappealing acquaintance)

OR

lose your (insert body part)?

GETTING PERSONAL

YOU MUST CHOOSE!

Would you rather...

watch (insert two unattractive acquaintances) have sex

OR

get a lap dance by (insert friend's parent)?

Would you rather...

have (insert friend or relative) pose naked until you have painted a reasonably accurate portrait

OR

meticulously moisturize, massage, and talc (insert unattractive person)?

Would you rather...

engage in heavy petting with (insert head of state)

OR

dry hump (insert political satirist)?

Would you rather...

play (insert board game) with (insert hot celebrity)

OR

(insert verb) with a (insert adjective) (insert former San Diego Charger wide receiver)?

GETTING PERSONAL

YOU MUST CHOOSE!

Would you rather...

share an eighteen hour car ride with (insert annoying acquaintance)

OR

put on (insert friend)'s socks every day for a month?

Would you...

have sex with (insert someone repulsive) to have sex with (insert someone desirable)?

Would you rather...

bathe and powder (insert disgusting acquaintance) twice a day every day for a week?

OR

slap a full nelson on (insert friend's mother) for five minutes?

Would you rather...

see (insert attractive acquaintance) naked

OR

see (someone you hate) wounded?

Would you rather...

take a tour of Vermont's covered bridges with (insert famous dictator)

OR

play Connect Four with (insert famous artist)?

GETTING PERSONAL

CHAPTER 1 2

THE DEITY'S GREATEST HITS: VOLUME II: ELECTRIC BOOGALOO

The Deity's been sniffing glue again. He's set to random play again, and there's no telling what kind of dilemma may show up.

YOU MUST CHOOSE!

Would you rather...

walk like an eighty year old

OR

a two year old?

Would you rather...

have confederate flag irises *OR* Velcro body hair

erasers for lips *OR* corkscrews for pinky fingernails?

mayonnaise tears *OR* Koolaid sweat?

Would you rather...

have breast implants made of sculpting clay OR cedar shavings?

Legos OR hydrogen?

bleu cheese OR live crickets?

glow-in-the-dark silly putty OR rice?

dark matter OR the soul of Terrance Trent D'Arby?

Would you rather...

turn into Sammy Davis Jr. when masturbating

OR

have the AOL "you've got mail" guy announce your ejaculations?

THE DEITY'S GREATEST HITS: VOLUME II: ELECTRIC BOOGALOO

YOU MUST CHOOSE!

The Deity has imprisoned you in a closed room. You are in a fight to the death. All enemies are hostile.

Would you rather fight...

a tiger with no front legs *OR* 800 bullfrogs?

3000 butterflies *OR* 1 bobcat?

Lawrence Taylor *OR* the cast of the Wonder Years?

10 Phil Donahues *OR* 3 Chuck Norrises?

300 remote control cars *OR* 30 sentient red rubber playground balls?

Would you rather...

have sex with a 10 *OR* two 5's? (5's are at the same time)

a 10 *OR* ten 1's?

a 10 with syphilis *OR* a 4 with nice high thread count sheets?

a 10 and a -3 *OR* a 5?

Siamese twin 10's *OR* just one 10?

$10^2 - (2 + \sqrt{125/9})$ *OR* $2^{4(32 - .65)}$

Things to consider: order of operations

YOU MUST CHOOSE!

Would you rather...

emit steam from your ears when you're angry
OR
exude Tang from your hands when you're tardy?

Would you have sex with...

a bearded Paris Hilton *OR* a breaded Christina Applegate?

Glenn Close *OR* a three-times-the-normal-density Catherine Zeta Jones?

Rebecca Lobo *OR* an eight month pregnant Elizabeth Hurley?

the sublime Lynn Redgrave *OR* the subliming Vicki Lawrence?

YOU MUST CHOOSE!

Would you rather...

have a reverse digestive tract?

OR

conduct all written work in the voice of Snoop Doggy Dogg?

Would you rather...

menstruate Yoo-Hoo

OR

have hot fudge post-nasal drip?
Things to consider: weight gain

THE DEITY'S GREATEST HITS: VOLUME II: ELECTRIC BOOGALOO

YOU MUST CHOOSE!

Would you rather...

be only able to see yourself through Ernest Hemingway's eyes

OR

have self-esteem dependent upon your proximity to granite quarries?

Things to consider: Hemingway's strict demands for machismo, quarry groupies

Would you rather...

have the ability to silence with a stare

OR

goose with a wink?

Would you rather...

have a head that reflects light like a disco party ball

OR

puff up like a blowfish when you sense danger?

Would you rather...

have phone sex with the teacher from the old Charlie Brown specials

OR

have telegraph sex? (see below for example)

PHONE SEX OPERATOR: I'm so horny STOP

YOU: What are you wearing STOP

PHONE SEX OPERATOR: Nothing STOP I'm so horny STOP

YOU: Oh yeah? STOP... (silence) No, I mean, don't stop. STOP... (silence)... Crap...

YOU MUST CHOOSE!

Would you rather...

be unable to understand the written word unless read to you by *Dukes of Hazzard* star Tom Wopat

OR

have your legal name changed to "Doo-Doo McGee"?

Things to consider: office staff meetings, contract signings

Would you rather...

be able to fly but be afraid of heights

OR

be able to become invisible but be a compulsive masturbator?

YOU MUST CHOOSE!

Would you rather...
ejaculate hot coffee
OR
crazy glue?

Would you rather...
have the peripheral vision of Magic Johnson
OR
the magic vision of Peripheral Johnson? (work in progress)

Would you rather...

have to communicate solely in baby talk

OR

in *Three's Company* style double entendre?

Would you rather...

have breasts that age ten times faster than the rest of your body

OR

have no feeling whatsoever in your genital regions, except when touched by people over the age of 90?

Would you rather...

have a toilet that bucked like a bronco

OR

a bigoted toaster oven?

Would you rather...

be incapable of closing your eyes at the same time

OR

have three children, all named Marshall?

YOU MUST CHOOSE!

Extra Credit: (Left-overs)

Would you rather...

have to wear clothes of airplane fabric clothing, have four knuckle fingers, pronounce every third word "kelbor", be allergic to Don Mattingly, and have a breeze that perpetually blows by making your hair look healthy and manageable like models'

OR

have to play all sports holding hands with Gil Gerard, speak like an 18th century British dowager, be shrouded in fog, age to 40 then reverse, and always feel like you do when you bite into an ice-cold popsicle with your most sensitive teeth?

Would you rather...

have Gary Coleman's face for pupils

OR

be limited to cleansing yourself by use of a DustBuster?

Would you rather...

only be sexually aroused by people experiencing engine trouble

OR

having severe allergic reactions?

YOU MUST CHOOSE!

Would you rather...

have nipples that roved and wandered all over your body

OR

have hair that changes color and falls out in the autumn?

Would you rather...

be sexually abused by Count Chocula

OR

get bukkaked by the Smurfs?

Would you rather...

see the world in Atari 2600 graphic quality

OR

in the perspective and outlook of the most jaded Hollywood agent in America?

Would you rather...

be incapable of moving your body once sexually turned on

OR

be completely infertile except when inside churches?

THE DEITY'S GREATEST HITS: VOLUME II: ELECTRIC BOOGALOO

Would you rather...

perpetually feel like you're walking through cobwebs

OR

have sandy insides?

Would you rather...

perpetually feel the annoyance and embarrassment when they sing Happy Birthday to you at a crowded restaurant

OR

the frustration of the fifteenth minute looking for your keys?

Would you rather...

walk like an Egyptian

OR

date a girl with an unwavering propensity to party all the time?

Upon climax, would you rather...

shout out the names of various US Presidents *OR* Zagat's restaurant reviews?

the chorus to "Hava Nagila" *OR* the chorus to "Whoomp! There It Is"?

Would You Rather...? questions *OR* Barry Larkin's career statistics?

YOU MUST CHOOSE!

Would you rather...

have sex with Diana Ross *OR* a 200% scale Denise Richards?

Maria Bartiromo *OR* a blurry Adriana Lima?

a drunk Tara Reid *OR* a Jennifer Love Hewitt who won't shut up about her trip to Sea World?

Will Smith after undergoing a sex change *OR* Sarah Michelle Gellar 10 seconds after she gives birth?

everyone you know with a surname starting with "B" *OR* "W"?

Josh Hartnett *OR* Gary Coleman if they exchanged heights?

Hugh Grant *OR* Mr. T if they switched voices and demeanors?

Would you rather...

be the Supreme Court Justices' sex slave for a day

OR

be wagon-trained by a pack of oompa-loompas?

Would you rather...

vomit dice

OR

excrete Monopoly real estate?

THE DEITY'S GREATEST HITS: VOLUME II: ELECTRIC BOOGALOO

YOU MUST CHOOSE!

Would you rather...

have high-voltage body hair

OR

have skin covered in photos of Vernon Maxwell?

Would you rather...

have an irresistible compulsion to lick your throwing hand's thumb like a quarterback every few seconds

OR

have to have 1 hand on your crotch at all times (that hand doesn't have to belong to you)?

Would you rather...

breathe to the rhythm of "Eine Kleine Nacht Musik" by Mozart

OR

have your first born look exactly like Harold Ramis?

Would you rather...

be able to hear every cell phone ring in your neighborhood

OR

smell every fart?

YOU MUST CHOOSE!

Would you rather...

have a harmonica implanted in your nasal passageway

OR

have all your memories eventually fade into the tone of rap videos?

Would you rather...

urinate crazy string

OR

lactate grits?

YOU MUST CHOOSE!

Would you rather...

have your face on the national currency

OR

your ass on it?

Would you rather...

have sex in front of your grandparents

OR

the *American Idol* judges?

YOU MUST CHOOSE!

Would you rather...

have the flexibility of one of those bendy toys

OR

have freckles on your body that shift to mimic the movement of the constellations?

Would you rather...

be able to type the phrase "Kesselman stole my matzoh!" at the astonishing rate of 1,500 words a minute

OR

be capable of accurately guessing the amount of days between any two people's birthdays without knowing the actual date of either?

Things to consider: convincing primitive peoples you are a god

---

WOULD YOU RATHER...?

Would you rather...

experience a brain freeze (literally) *OR* heart break (literally)?

have porcelain skin (literally) *OR* hair of gold (literally)?

have the eye of the tiger (literally) *OR* broccoli pubic hair (literally)?

Would you rather have your only means of foreplay be...

cheek-kissing *OR* joint-fondling?

firm handshakes *OR* the ferocious tonguing of eyeballs?

political debate *OR* *Three's Company*-like misunderstandings?

YOU MUST CHOOSE!

Would you rather be stuck on a desert island with...

the complete works of Jane Austen *OR* a year's worth of *Barely Legal*?

your significant other and an Ipod filled with Barry White's most sultry tunes *OR* your significant other and a complete set of *Magic: The Gathering* cards?

a fishing rod *OR* a funhouse mirror, a wig, and some KY jelly?

Socrates *OR* Jenna Jameson?

P-Diddy's wardrobe *OR* an unlimited supply of nude photos of Tony Feuerstein?

For thirty seconds, would you rather...

lie down naked on a Benihana table

OR

have your mouth stretched around the part of a lawnmower where the grass spits out while it mows high grass?

Would you rather...

have charming dimples but have to forever and exclusively use the email address scrotiescrote@hotmail.com

OR

have a twinkle in your eye, but be engaged to someone that swears s/he is the reincarnation of Oliver Cromwell (and passes a lie detector test to prove it)?

YOU MUST CHOOSE!

Would you rather have your dreams written and directed by...

Quentin Tarantino *OR* Woody Allen?

Ed Wood *OR* the creators of *Desperate Housewives*?

Spike Lee *OR* Stan Lee?

John Hughes *OR* Ron Jeremy?

Would you rather...

drool Drain-O

OR

exhale Raid?

Answer Keys

Answers to This or That?

1) a. NHL b. H.O. c. H.O. d. NHL

2) a. nazi (Rommel) b. book c. nazi (Mengele) d. book

3a) a. porn star b. weather term c. weather term d. porn star

3b) a. meteorologist b. porn term c. both

4) a. Tandy film b. euphemism c. Tandy film d. euphemism

5) a. chieftain b. euphemism c. euphemism d. neither

Answers to Spell Check Quiz

1. Cyanide Pauper – Cyndi Lauper
2. Simian Believer – Simon Bolivar
3. Fabliau, phobia, FBI - Fabio
4. Jason Boatmen – Jason Bateman
5. Lays Milan – Alyssa Milano
6. Elite Gourd – Eliot Gould
7. Cedar, Pig – Pia Zadora

Answers to This or That?

1. a. Supreme Court Justice   b. Venereal Disease   c. Venereal Disease
   d. Supreme Court Justice

2. a. Bible Chapter   b. Porn Magazine   c. Both   d. Porn Magazine

3. a. Batman Villain   b. Dildo   c. Batman Villain   d. Dildo

4. a. VD Symptom   b. Catskills Comedian   c. VD Symptom
   d. Catskills Comedian

Answers to Pornification

1. American Beauty
2. City Slickers
3. Finding Nemo
4. The Slutty Professor
5. T.W.A.T
6. Sex Toy Story or Boy Story
7. Big Trouble in Little Vagina
8. Analize This
9. Glory Hole
10. Face Jam
11. Malcolm XXX
12. Titty Titty Gang Bang
13. Shaft
14. Cold Mountin'
15. Lou Dobbs Money Shot

Answers to Mystery Quiz

1. Malted milk balls
2. 200 mg
3. False
4. Ed Begley, Jr.
5. Ed Begley, Sr.
6. No, thank you.
7. See 1, 4.

Coming Soon: Other *Would You Rather...?* books by the authors

Wouldn't You Rather...: Over 200 Pointed Questions to Answer

Sample question: **Wouldn't you rather...** go to the beach than the mountains?

Things to consider: I mean, really, it's obvious, isn't it? Sub? Surf? Jeez!

Would You Rather...? Australia

Sample question: **Would you rather...** take a walkabout with bunyips sand yowies in nothing but your stubbies OR get in a barney with a fair-dinkum yobbo?

Things to consider: chooks, dunny-buggies

Would You Rather...? Mormon Edition

Sample question: **Would you rather...** marry a Mormon spouse, thereby sealing your eternal place in the Celestial Kingdom OR be allowed to drink coffee?

About the Authors

Justin Heimberg is an author and screenwriter living in suburban Maryland.

David Gomberg is whitish-blue in color but pulses with a reddish glow from the heat his body produces. The creature is a little more than 20 feet long, with a body about 5 feet wide. It weighs about 10,000 pounds. Gomberg cannot speak. Gomberg hides under the snow and ice until he hears movement above him, then attacks from below and surprises prey. When Gomberg begins his turn with a grappled opponent in his mouth, he can swallow that opponent with a successful grapple check. Once inside, the opponent takes 2d8+12 points of bludgeoning damage plus 8d6 points of fire damage per round from Gomberg's gizzard. Gomberg's interior can hold 2 Large, 4 Medium, 8 Small, 32 Tiny, 128 Diminutive, or 512 Fine or smaller opponents.

About the Deity

The ringmaster/MC/overlord of the *Would You Rather...* empire is "the Deity." Psychologically and physically a cross between Charles Manson and Gabe Kaplan, the Deity is the one responsible for creating and presenting the WYR dilemmas. It is the Deity who asks "Would you rather...watch a porno movie with your parents or a porno movie starring your parents?" And it is the Deity who orders, without exception, that you must choose. No one knows exactly why he does this; suffice to say, it's for reasons beyond your understanding. The Deity communicates with you not through speech, nor telepathy, but rather through several sharp blows to the stomach that vary in power and location. Nearly omnipotent, often ruthless, and obsessed with former NBA seven-footers, the Deity is a random idea generator with a peculiar predilection for intervening in your life in the strangest ways.